First Graphic Organizers:
Reading

30 Reproducible Graphic Organizers That Build Early Reading and Comprehension Skills

by Rhonda Graff Silver

NEW YORK • TORONTO • LONDON • AUCKLAND • SYDNEY
MEXICO CITY • NEW DELHI • HONG KONG • BUENOS AIRES

To Scott, Craig and Daniel,
and to all children whose learning differences
make them wonderfully unique.

With thanks to my colleagues Holly Sandler, Mi Jung An, Pam Buck,
Julia Singer and Kelly Chasanoff for their feedback, advice and friendship.

And thanks to my students, who have taught me so much about teaching, listening
and understanding. And a special thank you to my editor, Kama Einhorn.

Cover design by Jim Sarfati
Interior design by Solutions by Design, Inc.
Interior illustrations by Rusty Fletcher and Teresa Anderko

ISBN: 0-439-45828-5

Copyright 2003 by Rhonda Graff Silver
All rights reserved. Published by Scholastic Inc.
Printed in the U.S.A.

2 3 4 5 6 7 8 9 10   40   09 08 07 06 05 04 03

Contents

Introduction

WHY GRAPHIC ORGANIZERS?

"A graphic organizer is a visual representation of knowledge."
— Bromley, Irwin-DeVito, and Modlo

Graphic organizers allow children to make sense of information. Perfect for visual learners, they provide children with a place to start, help them focus on key points, and help structure their thinking, allowing them to remember and understand what they read and hear. They help children organize ideas and concepts into a meaningful visual, which is easier to remember than a long piece of text. Using graphic organizers also helps enhance group discussion. And, they can be used with almost any book!

USING THIS BOOK

The graphic organizers are arranged into the following categories: pre-reading, character, sequencing, main idea, vocabulary, reading response, and nonfiction. Use them however and whenever they work for you and your class! Each organizer includes a teacher page explaining the organizer's benefits, a materials list, an indication of when to use it, step-by-step suggestions for use, and discussion starters. In addition, helpful tips for adapting each organizer are included. Each organizer is also shown completed for your reference and inspiration. (See page 6.)

On each organizer, children have ample space to write and draw. Drawing is a way that many children are able to express their knowledge. Some children may be more comfortable drawing prior to, in conjunction with, or after writing. Encourage varied responses and use discussion to expand upon what children write or draw. Remember, as children learn to think about what they read, their responses will gradually become more sophisticated and insightful.

4

There is no right or wrong way to use these organizers! They can be used to help children of different ability levels and in different ways. They can be used for whole group, small group or independent response. Initially, you might recreate the organizers on chart paper and model the process to the group, then display the enlarged copy for further reference. Model how to use the organizer and encourage discussion focused on specific aspects of the organizer. By modeling and sharing your thought processes out loud, children will learn how to use the organizers more independently over time.

Discussion questions are included for all the organizers. Use them as suggestions (your goals and children's abilities should be your guide). Because there are multiple ways to complete each organizer, discussion and understanding should be the focus. Encourage children to talk about their thinking. Asking children to elaborate on a thought or to explain *why* often develops a deeper understanding on his or her part, as well as the rest of the group.

You can use the organizers to make assessments (formal and informal), adjusting your teaching to the level of children's understanding. Of course, from time to time you'll want to evaluate how the organizers are working. How are children improving? Are they moving along as readers, and "explorers" of language? Are they inquisitive? What kinds of learners are they becoming? How can the organizers be used to meet the varied needs of the group?

And last—have fun! Graphic organizers provide an exciting avenue to explore comprehension and develop a love of reading! This book offers you a great beginning in using organizers with young children. Let your experience and your children's questions and responses take you the rest of the way. No two teachers will have the same journey, but we can continue to share our professional experiences in order to enhance children's understanding and enjoyment of reading, writing, and sharing.

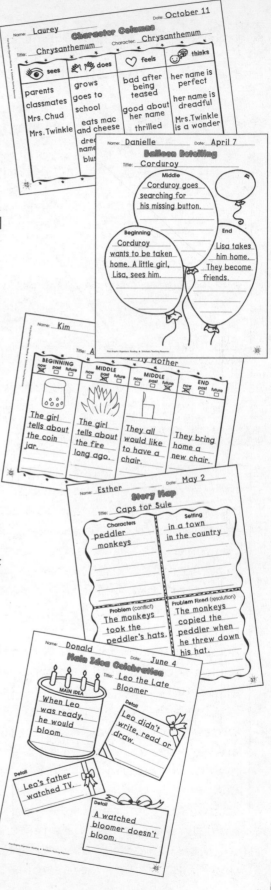

IN EACH UNIT

For each of the 30 organizers, you'll find...

An at-a-glance materials list and indicator of when to use the organizer.

A brief description of the organizer's benefits.

An indication of whether the organizer is for pre-reading, teaching character, exploring sequencing, teaching main idea, teaching vocabulary, encouraging reading response, or teaching nonfiction.

An example of a completed organizer.

Ready-to-reproduce pages.

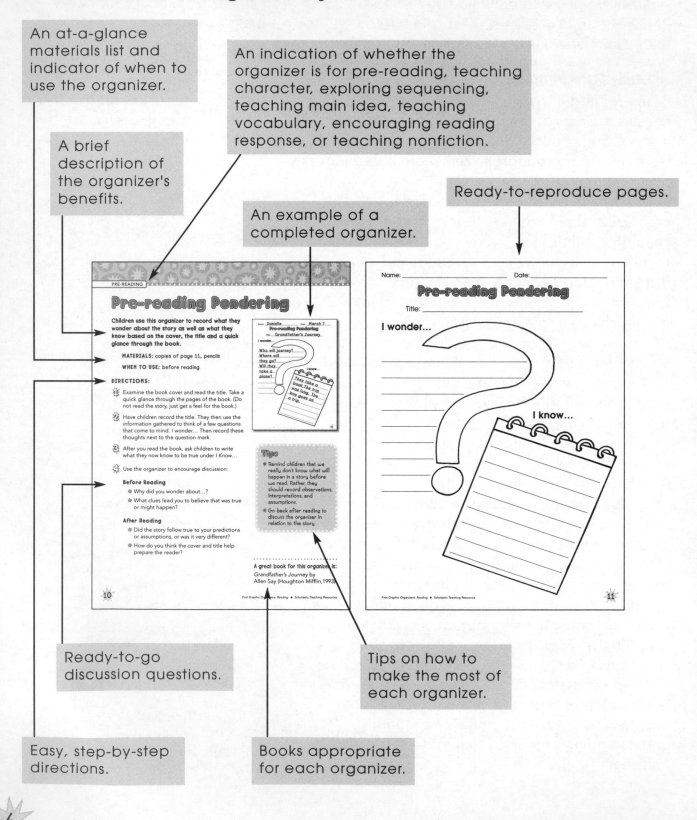

Ready-to-go discussion questions.

Easy, step-by-step directions.

Books appropriate for each organizer.

Tips on how to make the most of each organizer.

MEETING THE LANGUAGE ARTS STANDARDS

The graphic organizers in this book are designed to support you in meeting the following standards outlined by the Mid-Continent Regional Educational Laboratory (MCREL), an organization that collects and synthesizes national and state K-12 curriculum standards.

Reading: Grades K-2

Uses the general skills and strategies of the reading process

✳ Understands that print conveys meaning (i.e., knows that printed letters and words represent spoken language)

✳ Understands how print is organized and read (e.g., identifies front and back covers, title page, author, and illustrator; follows words from left-to-right and from top-to-bottom; knows the significance of spaces between words, knows the difference between letters, words, and sentences; understands the use of capitalization and punctuation as text boundaries)

✳ Creates mental images from pictures and print

✳ Uses meaning clues (e.g., pictures, picture captions, title, cover, headings, story structure, story topic) to aid comprehension and make predictions about content (e.g., action, events, character's behavior)

✳ Uses basic elements of phonetic analysis (e.g., common letter/sound relationships, beginning and ending consonants, vowel sounds, blends, word patterns) to decode unknown words

✳ Uses basic elements of structural analysis (e.g., syllables, basic prefixes, suffixes, root words, compound words, spelling patterns, contractions) to decode unknown words

✳ Uses a picture dictionary to determine word meaning

✳ Understands level-appropriate sight words and vocabulary (e.g., words for persons, places, things, actions; high frequency words such as said, was, and where)

✳ Uses self-correction strategies (e.g., searches for cues, identifies miscues, rereads, asks for help)

✳ Reads aloud familiar stories, poems, and passages with fluency and expression (e.g., rhythm, flow, meter, tempo, pitch, tone, intonation)

* Uses reading skills and strategies to understand and interpret a variety of literary texts

* Uses reading skills and strategies to understand a variety of familiar literary passages and texts (e.g., fairy tales, folktales, fiction, nonfiction, legends, fables, myths, poems, nursery rhymes, picture books, predictable books)

* Knows setting, main characters, main events, sequence, and problems in stories

* Makes simple inferences regarding the order of events and possible outcomes

* Knows the main ideas or theme of a story

* Relates stories to personal experiences (e.g., events, characters, conflicts, themes)

Uses reading skills and strategies to understand and interpret a variety of informational texts

* Uses reading skills and strategies to understand a variety of informational texts (e.g., written directions, signs, captions, warning labels, informational books)

* Understands the main idea and supporting details of simple expository information

* Summarizes information found in texts (e.g., retells in own words)

* Relates new information to prior knowledge and experience

The Graphic Organizers

Pre-reading Pondering

Children use this organizer to record what they wonder about the story as well as what they know based on the cover, the title and a quick glance through the book.

MATERIALS: copies of page 11, pencils

WHEN TO USE: before reading

DIRECTIONS:

1. Examine the book cover and read the title. Take a quick glance through the pages of the book. (Do not read the story, just get a feel for the book.)

2. Have children record the title. They then use the information gathered to think of a few questions that come to mind. *I wonder…* Then record these thoughts next to the question mark.

3. After you read the book, ask children to write what they now know to be true under *I Know…*

4. Use the organizer to encourage discussion:

Before Reading

* Why did you wonder about…?
* What clues lead you to believe that was true or might happen?

After Reading

* Did the story follow true to your predictions or assumptions, or was it very different?
* How do you think the cover and title help prepare the reader?

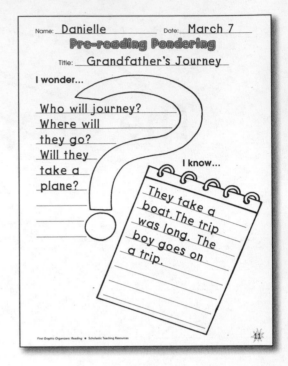

Name: Danielle   Date: March 7

Pre-reading Pondering

Title: Grandfather's Journey

I wonder…

Who will journey?
Where will they go?
Will they take a plane?

I know…

They take a boat. The trip was long. The boy goes on a trip.

First Graphic Organizers: Reading ● Scholastic Teaching Resources   11

Tips

* Remind children that we really don't know what will happen in a story before we read. Rather, they should record observations, interpretations, and assumptions.

* Go back after reading to discuss the organizer in relation to the story.

A great book for this organizer is:

Grandfather's Journey by Allen Say (Houghton Mifflin, 1993)

Name: _____ Date: _____

Pre-reading Pondering

Title: _____

I wonder...

_____

_____

_____

_____

_____

_____

_____

I know...

Think It Over

Children use the title and pictures of a book to recall situations they've experienced.

MATERIALS: copies of page 13, pencils, crayons

WHEN TO USE: before reading

DIRECTIONS:

1. Look at the book, read the title, and note the cover illustration. Take a quick look through the book, noting any special illustrations. (For chapter books with fewer illustrations, note chapter titles.) Have children record the title on the lines.

2. Encourage children to think about how what they have seen or heard from the book relates to their own lives. *Does the title remind you of anything? Do the pictures make you think about anything in your own life?*

3. Encourage children to write their responses in the top box.

4. Children use the bottom four boxes to record words that come to mind when they think about the topic.

5. Use the organizer to encourage discussion:

   - Have children share their illustration and briefly tell about its relation to the story.

   - Have children share the words they wrote. Ask, *Why did you choose that word? How does it connect to the story?*

Tips

* When encouraging children to record responses, allow them to choose between written and illustrated responses. Or, they may choose to respond both ways.

* Help children label or provide captions for the illustrations.

A great book for this organizer is:

The Relatives Came by Cynthia Rylant (Macmillan, 1985)

Name: _____   Date: _____

Think It Over

Title: _____

Read the title and skim the book.

What I think about when I read the title:

Words I think about
before I read:

Predict & Check

Children will make predictions before and during reading, then confirm or correct their predictions after they read.

MATERIALS: copies of page 15, pencils, crayons

WHEN TO USE: before, during, and after reading

DIRECTIONS:

1 Have children record the title. Take a quick look through the book and have children make a first prediction. Have children write the prediction on the lines in box A1 and record the page number. Space is provided to illustrate as well.

2 Begin or continue reading until an appropriate prediction point. Have children make a second prediction and write it on the lines in box B1. They can then record the page number and illustrate.

3 Continue reading until the end, then go back and have children reread their predictions. Help children complete the *After Reading* column. (Children reread prediction A1 and record and illustrate the actual happenings in box A2, then do the same for prediction B1.)

4 Use the organizer to encourage discussion:
  * What clues did you use to make your predictions?
  * How accurate were your predictions?
  * Why is it a good reading strategy to predict as you read?

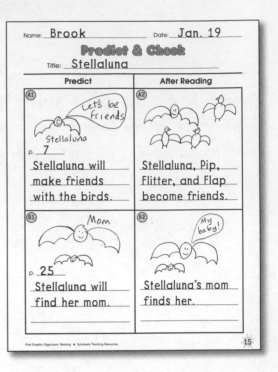

Tip

* Identify the prediction points prior to distributing the pages.

A great book for this organizer is:

Stellaluna by Janell Cannon (Harcourt Brace, 1993)

Name: _____   Date: _____

Predict & Check

Title: _____

Predict	After Reading

(A1)

p. _____

_____

_____

_____

(A2)

p. _____

_____

_____

_____

(B1)

p. _____

_____

_____

_____

(B2)

p. _____

_____

_____

_____

The Proof Is in the Character

Children will make inferences about a character, providing proof from the story to support their conclusions.

MATERIALS: copies of page 17, pencils, crayons

WHEN TO USE: during reading, at end of book

DIRECTIONS:

1. Have children choose a character from the story and write the character's name in the box labeled "character's name." They can then draw the character.

2. Have children identify character traits based on what they read. They then list these traits next to A and B.

3. Have children go back in the story to find specific parts that show, support, or prove why the character exhibits the given trait. They record the proof on the corresponding lines, A and B.

4. Have children illustrate in the boxes provided.

5. Use the organizer to encourage discussion:

   - How do you feel this trait helps or hinders the character in the story?
   - Is the trait positive or negative?
   - What is the connection between the trait and the proof?
   - Do you possess any traits similar to this character?
   - What traits would you use to identify yourself?

Tips

* Provide a short explanation of traits prior to using this organizer. Discuss specific children's traits, to personalize the concept.

* Have children work in small groups to complete an organizer together.

A great book for this organizer is:
Poppleton by Cynthia Rylant (Scholastic, Blue Sky Press, 1997)

Name: _____

Date: _____

The Proof Is in the Character

Title: _____

Draw the character.

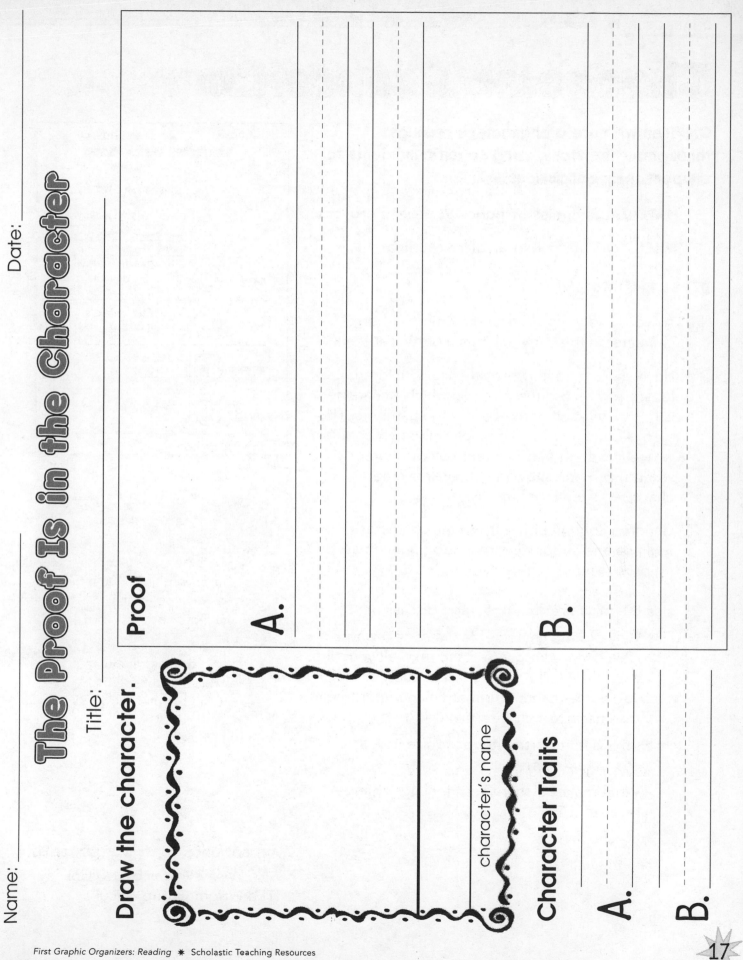

character's name

Character Traits

A. _____

B. _____

Proof

A. _____

B. _____

Character Connection

Children will note a character's feelings throughout the story, using specific incidents to support their conclusions.

MATERIALS: copies of page 19, pencils, crayons

WHEN TO USE: during or after reading

DIRECTIONS:

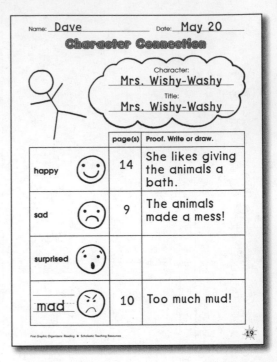

1 As you read, help children note times when a character in the story exhibits a particular feeling.

2 Have children record the title. Help children locate and record the page on which a character is happy. (Not all books have page numbers. This step is not critical, but it helps children recognize where information is in a text.) By drawing or writing, children show how they know the character is feeling that way.

3 Children continue identifying the character's feelings and supporting their judgments, based on proof from the story.

4 Use the organizer to encourage discussion:

 Why did the character feel a certain way? How do you know? (Did the text tell you, did you figure it out from an illustration, or did you gather other information and infer that the character felt a certain way?)

 Why is it important to recognize how a character feels?

🔅 What makes a character's feelings change over time?

Tips

✷ Provide a page number and have children identify the feelings of the character at that point in the story.

✷ Fill in the last line with a different character's feeling before distributing the handout.

A great book for this organizer is:
Mrs. Wishy-Washy by Joy Cowley (The Wright Group, 1980)

Name: _____   Date: _____

Character Connection

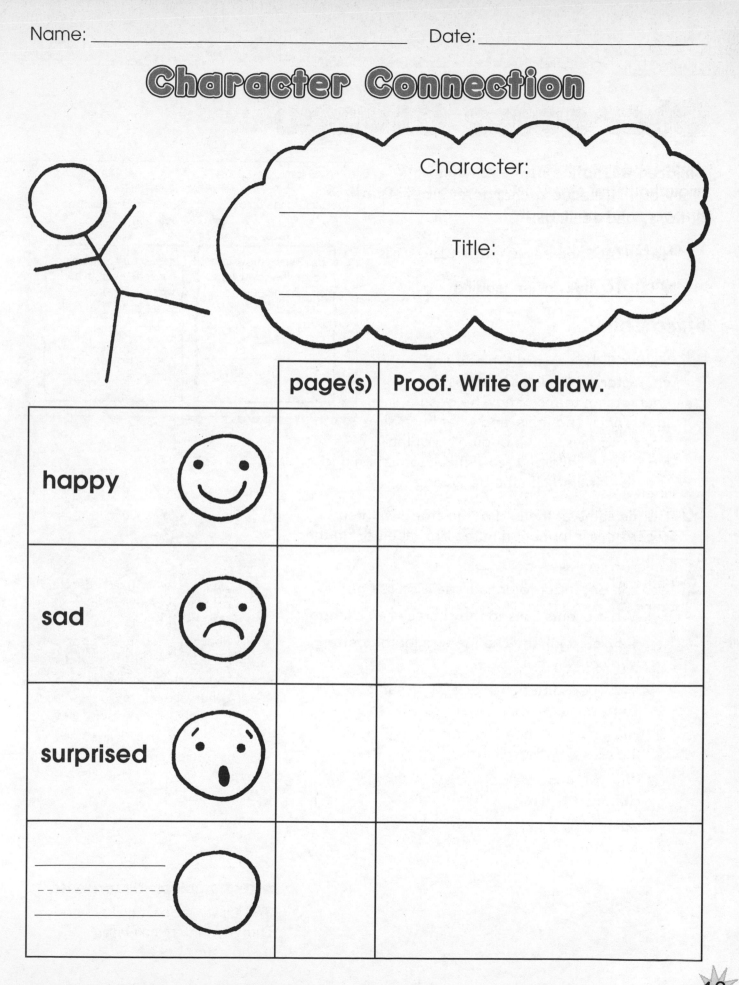

Character: _____

Title: _____

	page(s)	Proof. Write or draw.
happy		
sad		
surprised		
_____		

Character Change

Children will notice how events in a story can influence a character's beliefs, actions, and feelings.

MATERIALS: copies of page 21, pencils

WHEN TO USE: after reading

DIRECTIONS:

1 Have children record the title and character on the lines. Discuss the character in terms of how he or she looks, acts, and feels, and what he or she does and says, at the beginning of the story. Have children record this information under the box labeled, "In the beginning…"

2 Do the same at the end of the story. Children record this information in the box labeled, "In the end…"

3 Use the organizer to encourage discussion:

⚙ What events caused the character to change?

⚙ Do you think the change was for the better? Why or why not?

⚙ How does the behavior of the character impact the other characters?

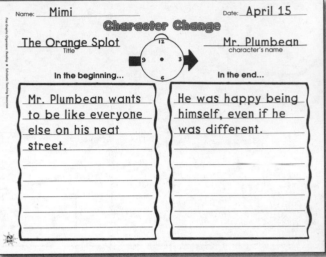

Name: Mimi	Date: April 15

Character Change

The Orange Splot	Mr. Plumbean
Title	character's name

In the beginning… | In the end…

| Mr. Plumbean wants to be like everyone else on his neat street. | He was happy being himself, even if he was different. |

Tip

✳ Elaborate on this organizer by creating a timeline of events showing how the character changes and how the changes impact the story as well as the other characters.

- -

A great book for this organizer is:

The Orange Splot by Daniel Manus Pinkwater (Scholastic, 1993)

Name: _____

Character Change

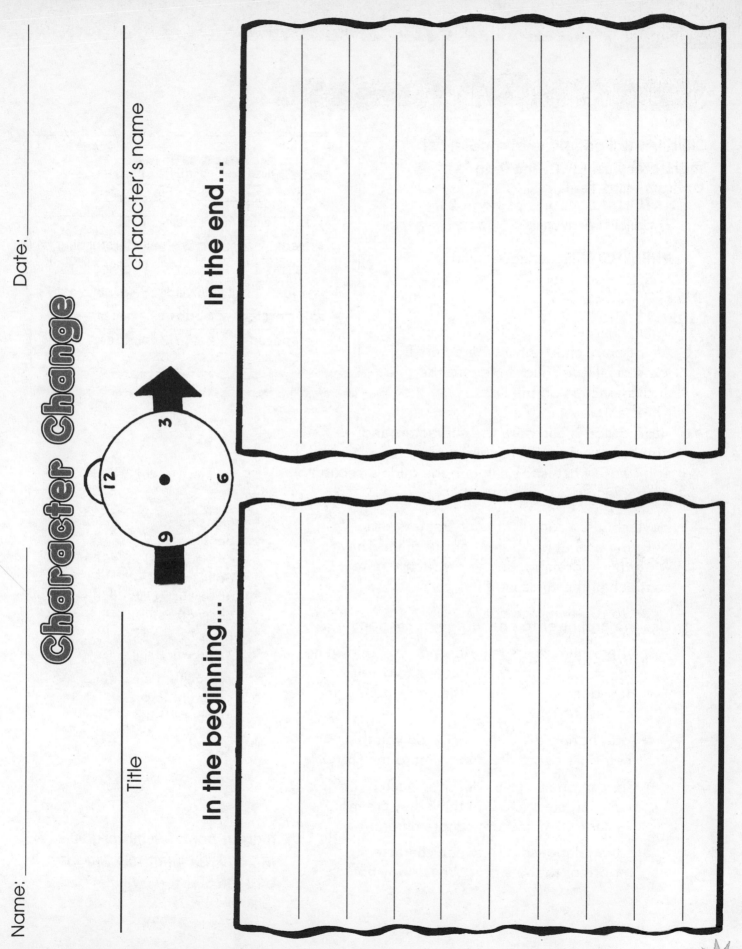

Title _____

character's name _____

In the beginning...

In the end...

Same & Different

Children will compare and contrast characters using a Venn Diagram.

MATERIALS: copies of page 23, pencils, crayons

WHEN TO USE: during reading, after reading

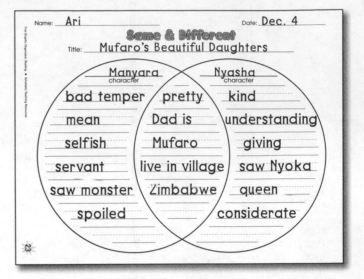

Name: Ari   Date: Dec. 4

Same & Different

Title: Mufaro's Beautiful Daughters

Manyara
character

Nyasha
character

bad temper — pretty — kind

mean — Dad is — understanding

selfish — Mufaro — giving

servant — live in village — saw Nyoka

saw monster — Zimbabwe — queen

spoiled — considerate

DIRECTIONS:

1 As a group, choose two characters from the story. Have children record the title and characters on the lines.

2 Have children compare the characters and determine what they have in common. They write what is the same in the middle section of the Venn diagram.

3 Have children contrast the characters and determine what is different about them. They write this information in the respective outer sections of the circles.

4 Use the organizer to encourage discussion:

- After noting the similarities, do you think it is important for these characters to be alike? How does it help make the story more interesting?

- After noting the differences, do you think their differences are important to the story?

- Choose one word to describe each of the two characters. Do you think they are more similar to each other or more different?

- Is the relationship between characters important to the story? Why or why not?

Tips

- Consider comparing and contrasting the same character at different points of the story, or at different points of the character's life.

- Fill in part of the organizer and let the children complete the rest in a small group or independently.

A great book for this organizer is:

Mufaro's Beautiful Daughters by John Steptoe (William Morrow, 1987)

Name: _____

Date: _____

Same & Different

Title: _____

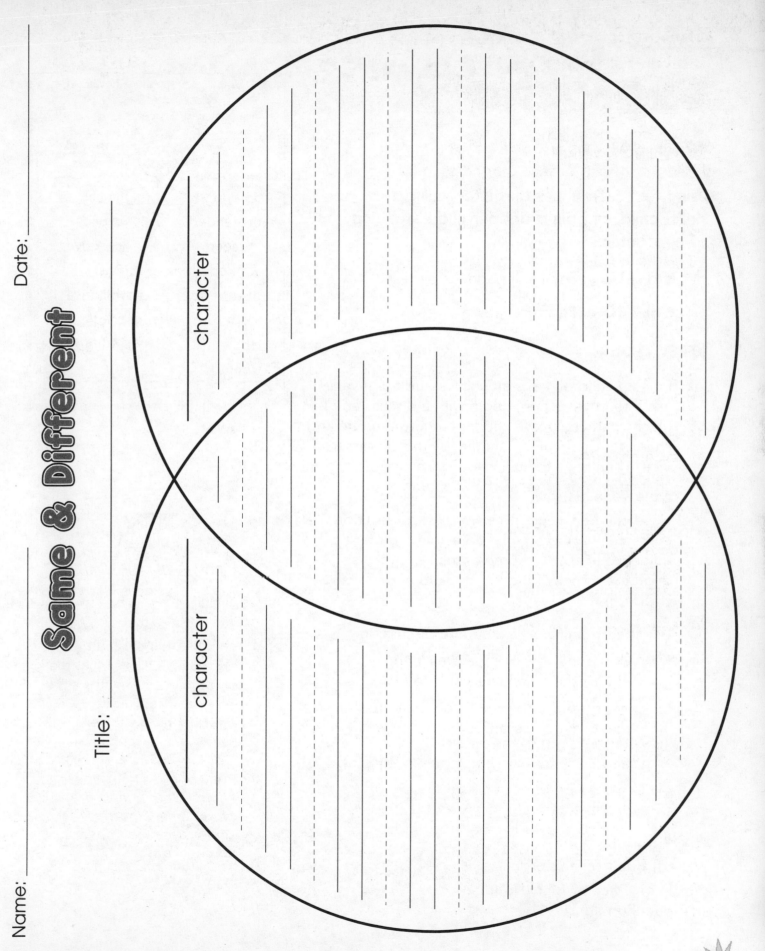

character

character

Character Report

Using text references and inferencing skills, children gain a deeper understanding of character.

MATERIALS: copies of page 25, pencils

WHEN TO USE: after reading

DIRECTIONS:

1. Be sure children have an understanding of verbs and adjectives. Then, begin with a discussion of a given character. Have children record the title and character on the lines, then draw the character's face. Then have them list specific actions of the character under the "verbs" heading.

2. Have children generate a word list to describe the character, recording the "adjectives" under the adjective heading. (Some of the descriptors might be directly from the book, but many will be inferred.)

3. Use the organizer to encourage discussion:

   ◉ What behaviors or situations in the story support the adjectives you chose?

   ◉ How do the verbs you listed relate to the adjectives you listed?

. . . .

A great book for this organizer is:
Amazing Grace by Mary Hoffman
(Penguin Putnam, 1991)

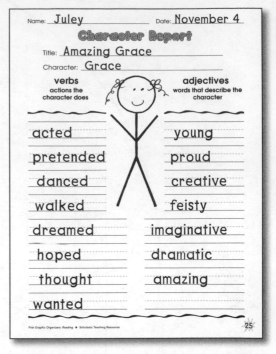

Name: **Juley**   Date: **November 4**

Character Report

Title: **Amazing Grace**

Character: **Grace**

verbs actions the character does	adjectives words that describe the character
acted	young
pretended	proud
danced	creative
walked	feisty
dreamed	imaginative
hoped	dramatic
thought	amazing
wanted	

First Graphic Organizers: Reading ● Scholastic Teaching Resources   25

Tip

✳ Provide simple scenarios to help develop inferencing skills. For example: *The girl ran into the room with a big smile. She raised her hands in the air and shouted, "Yes, we won!"* How did the girl feel? Explain to children that the text did not tell us the girl's feelings directly but we inferred from her behavior that she was happy. Say, *Let's look at the story we read and do the same thing for the character. How can we better understand and describe the character?*

Name: _____   Date: _____

Character Report

Title: _____

Character: _____

verbs
actions the
character does

adjectives
words that describe the
character

Character Columns

Children will analyze a character by identifying what he or she sees or does, feels and thinks throughout a story.

MATERIALS: copies of page 27, pencils

WHEN TO USE: during reading, after reading

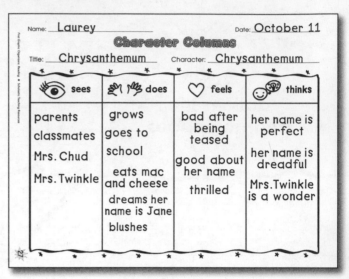

Name: Laurey			Date: October 11

Character Columns

Title: Chrysanthemum   Character: Chrysanthemum

👁 sees	🖐 does	♡ feels	☺ thinks
parents classmates Mrs. Chud Mrs. Twinkle	grows goes to school eats mac and cheese dreams her name is Jane blushes	bad after being teased good about her name thrilled	her name is perfect her name is dreadful Mrs. Twinkle is a wonder

DIRECTIONS:

1 Have children record the title. They then identify a focus character and record the character's name on the line at the top of the page.

2 Review the four columns. Begin by asking, *What are some things the character saw in this story?* Continue through each column in the same manner.

3 Have children write or draw what they remember.

4 Use the organizer to encourage discussion:

- How does what the character sees (does, feels, thinks) impact other characters in the story?

- How do the actions or feelings of the character change, if at all, in the story? What caused these changes?

Tips

* Have children work in groups and give each group a different character from the same story. Then have each group share their character analysis.

* This organizer can also help with pre-writing an autobiography or a biography.

A great book for this organizer is:

Chrysanthemum by Kevin Henkes (William Morrow & Company, 1991)

Name: _____

Date: _____

Character Columns

Character: _____

Title: _____

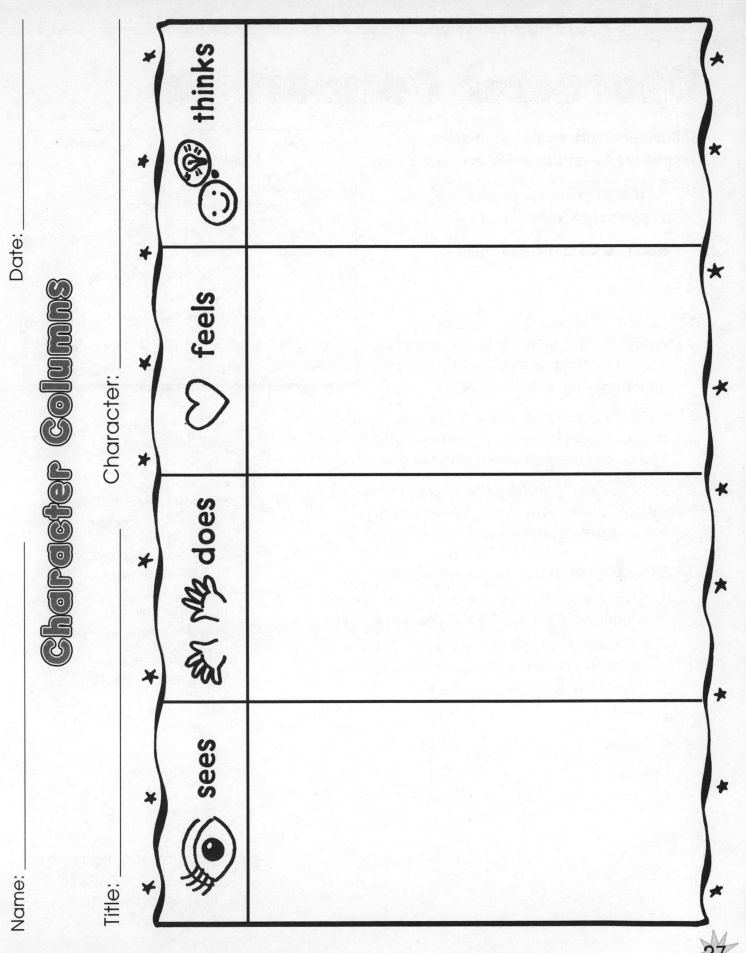

thinks	feels	does	sees

Character Comparison

Children compare and contrast themselves to a character in a story.

MATERIALS: copies of page 29, pencils, crayons

WHEN TO USE: after reading

DIRECTIONS:

1 Have children record a character's name on the line at the top of one circle. Then have them record their own name at the top of the other circle.

2 Have children ponder any differences between themselves and the chosen character, and record these differences in the outer circle.

3 Have children ponder any similarities they share with the chosen character, and record these similarities on the lines in the middle area.

4 Use the organizer to encourage discussion:

⚙ Do you think you share more similarities or more differences with this character? Why?

⚙ What type of relationship would you share with this character if you had the chance to meet? What makes you think this is true?

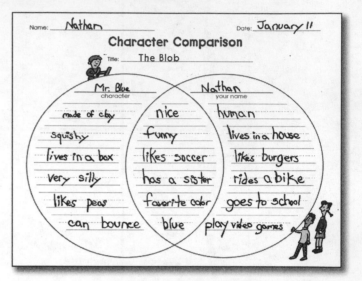

Name: Nathan   Date: January 11

Character Comparison

Title: The Blob

Mr. Blue (character) / Nathan (your name)

Mr. Blue	both	Nathan
made of clay	nice	human
squishy	funny	lives in a house
lives in a box	likes soccer	likes burgers
very silly	has a sister	rides a bike
likes peas	favorite color	goes to school
can bounce	blue	play video games

Tips

✳ Help children choose characters carefully so that they can relate to them in some way. However, it's fine if a child does not feel he or she has anything in common with a character. This might lead to an interesting discussion!

✳ Encourage children to respond using specific details.

A great book for this organizer is:

Wemberly Worried by Kevin Henkes (HarperCollins, 2000)

Name: _____

Date: _____

Character Comparison

Title: _____

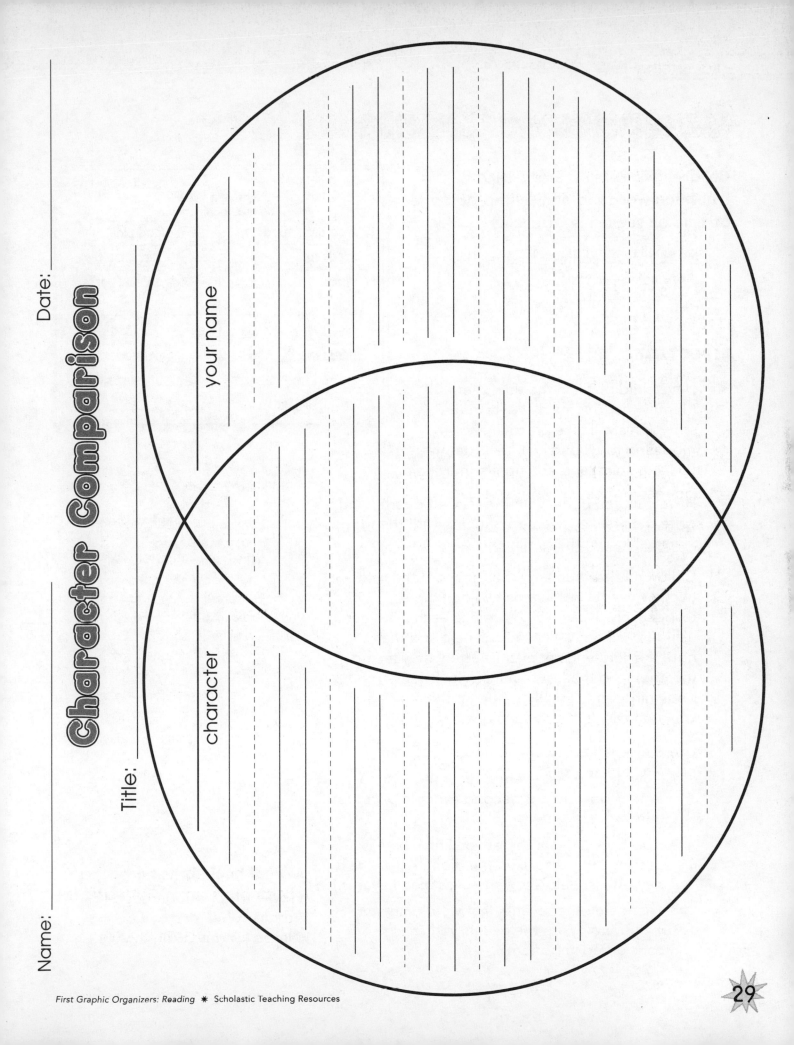

your name

character

Sequence Circle

Children will retell a story using transition words to convey the passage of time or sequence of events.

MATERIALS: copies of page 31, pencils, crayons

WHEN TO USE: after reading

DIRECTIONS:

1 Have children fill in the title, then identify the four main events in the story. (This will take practice and modeling for young children. Identifying the beginning and ending first may help.)

2 Have children begin with the top left quarter and write the first key event, beginning with the words "First…" or "In the beginning…"

3 Children follow the arrows and record the next two key events in sections two and three respectively. They should preface each statement using transition words such as *next* and *then* to note the sequence of events. Then, they record the ending in the last remaining quarter, beginning with "Finally…" or "In the end…" Children can illustrate each quarter.

4 Use the organizer to encourage discussion:

❂ How did the first event impact the second event? How did the second event impact the third?

❂ How does the author let you know time is passing? (Phrases like *That night, All the next day, At last* help show the passage of events.)

❂ There are other events that we did not include. Why are the events you chose considered important?

Tip

✳ Children may choose to illustrate before, or instead of, writing. This is a helpful way for many children to organize the sequence in their minds. They may then use the illustration to guide a verbal response.

A great book for this organizer is:

Frog and Toad Together by Arnold Lobel (HarperCollins, 1971)

Name: _____

Date: _____

Sequence Circle

Title: _____

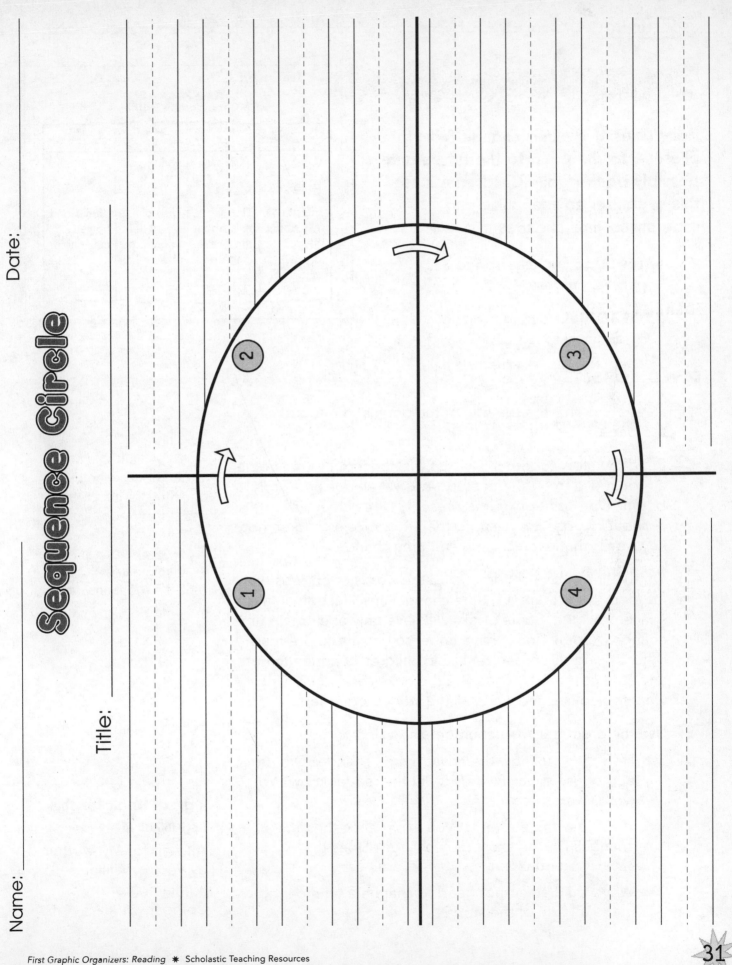

First Graphic Organizers: Reading ✴ Scholastic Teaching Resources

Time Passes

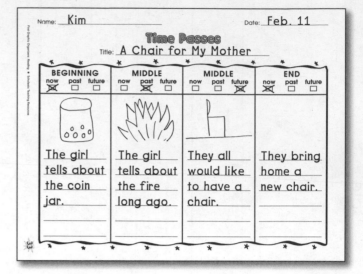

Many times story lines change from the present, to the past, to the future and possibly back again. Children will use this organizer to recognize and understand time changes in a story.

MATERIALS: copies of page 33, pencils, crayons

WHEN TO USE: during reading, after reading

DIRECTIONS:

1 Have children write the title of the book at the top of the page.

2 Read the story together. Discuss the concept of time frame as you move through the story. Ask, *When does the story begin? Does it begin in the present? Does it have a flashback? Does it move into the future?* Help children note key words that express time and time change.

3 On the lines, have children write the words or phrases that let them know there is a time change, and illustrate in the space provided. Some books will have only one or two time changes. (Some books have none, so be sure to pre-read before using this organizer.) Help children continue to note any time changes by checking the boxes and identifying what took place and when as the story progressed.

4 Use the organizer to encourage discussion:

  ◉ How did you know there was a time change? Did the author use special words to let the reader know? What words were used?

  ◉ How does the author let you experience the time change? Do the characters change? Does the setting change?

  ◉ Why would an author need to change a time period in the middle of the story?

Tip

✳ Tell children that the entire organizer may not be full. It will depend whether or not there are multiple time changes in the story.

A great book for this organizer is:

A Chair for My Mother by Vera B. Williams (William, Morrow & Company, 1982)

Name: _____

Date: _____

Time Passes

Title: _____

BEGINNING			MIDDLE			MIDDLE			END		
now ☐	past ☐	future ☐	now ☐	past ☐	future ☐	now ☐	past ☐	future ☐	now ☐	past ☐	future ☐

Balloon Retelling

Children will retell a story, using the structure of beginning, middle, and end.

MATERIALS: copies of page 35, pencils

WHEN TO USE: after reading

DIRECTIONS:

1 Together, identify the key points of the story. Decide on the important parts of the beginning. Children record this information in the "Beginning" balloon.

2 Help children complete the "Middle" balloon by writing or drawing about what took place in the middle of the story.

3 Children fill in the "End" balloon with information about the story's conclusion.

4 Use the organizer to encourage discussion:
  ✹ How did you decide what was important?
  ✹ Did the "Beginning" impact the "Middle" and "End" balloons?

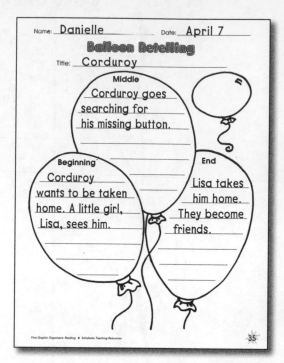

Name: Danielle   Date: April 7
Balloon Retelling
Title: Corduroy

Middle
Corduroy goes searching for his missing button.

Beginning
Corduroy wants to be taken home. A little girl, Lisa, sees him.

End
Lisa takes him home. They become friends.

First Graphic Organizers: Reading ✸ Scholastic Teaching Resources
35

Tips

✹ Have children change the ending, then discuss the differences between the real ending and the new ending.

✹ Provide the option of illustrating, rather than writing, the beginning, middle, and end of the story.

A great book for this organizer is:

Corduroy by Don Freeman (Viking Penguin, 1968)

Name: _____   Date: _____

Balloon Retelling

Title: _____

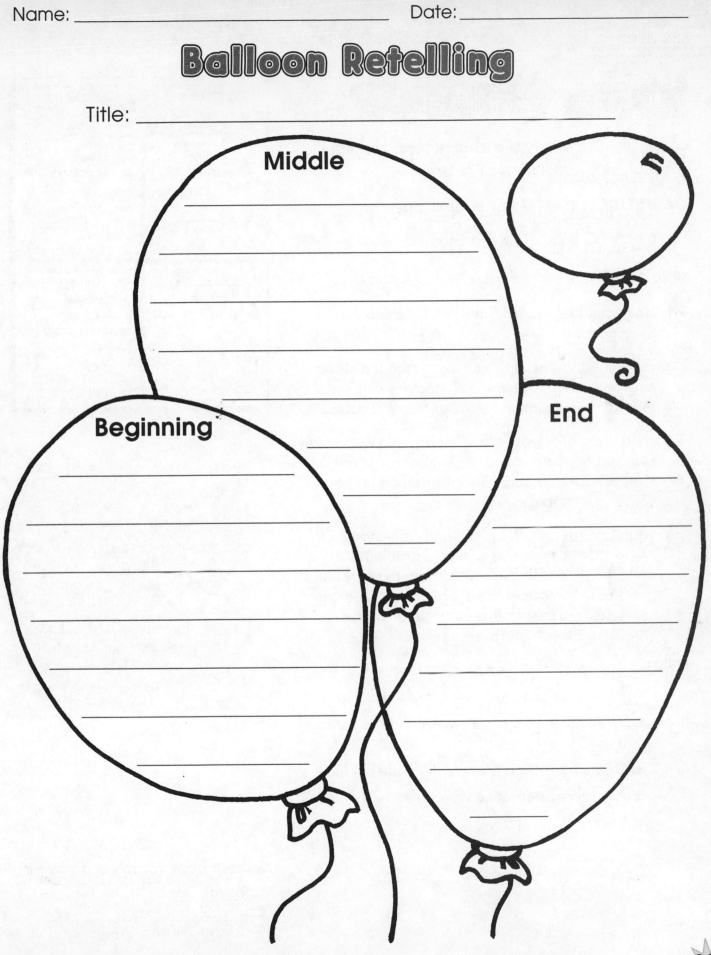

Middle
_____
_____
_____
_____
_____
_____
_____

Beginning
_____
_____
_____
_____
_____
_____

End
_____
_____
_____
_____
_____

Story Map

Children will identify the characters, setting, conflict, and resolution of a story.

MATERIALS: copies of page 37, pencils

WHEN TO USE: after reading

DIRECTIONS:

1 Have children record the title at the top of the page.

2 Help children recall the characters in the story and decide who the main characters are. They record information in the "Characters" bubble.

3 Help children identify the setting, and discuss the fact that the setting may change throughout the story. Children record this information in the "Setting" bubble.

4 Together, identify the problem of the story. (Be aware that not every story has a problem.) Children record this information in the "Problem" bubble. Discuss how the problem is solved and have children record this information in the "Problem Fixed" bubble.

5 Use the organizer to encourage discussion. Ask:

- ☼ What makes a character a main character?
- ☼ Which characters are involved in the conflict, if any?
- ☼ Does the setting play a role in the conflict?
- ☼ Are there alternative ways to solve the problem?

Name: **Esther**   Date: **May 2**

Story Map

Title: **Caps for Sale**

Characters	Setting
peddler	in a town
monkeys	in the country

Problem (conflict)	Problem Fixed (resolution)
The monkeys took the peddler's hats.	The monkeys copied the peddler when he threw down his hat.

First Graphic Organizers: Reading ● Scholastic Teaching Resources

37

Tips

✳ Model how to use organizer first (on chart paper or the board) so children are comfortable with the terms used.

✳ Children can illustrate and label the parts of the story before they start to use this organizer.

A great book for this organizer is:

Caps for Sale by Esphyr Slobodkina (Addison-Wesley, 1940)

Name: _____   Date: _____

Story Map

Title: _____

Characters

_____
_____
_____
_____
_____

Setting

_____
_____
_____
_____
_____

Problem (conflict)

_____
_____
_____
_____
_____

Problem Fixed (resolution)

_____
_____
_____
_____
_____

Beginning...Middle...End

Children will identify the beginning, middle, and end of a story.

> **MATERIALS:** copies of page 39, pencils, crayons

> **WHEN TO USE:** after reading

DIRECTIONS:

 1 Have children record the title. Then have them identify the key event that occurs at the beginning of the story. They can write it in the box labeled "In the beginning…"

2 Have children identify the key event that occurs in the middle of the story, and complete the box labeled "In the middle…"

3 Have the children identify the key event that occurs at the end of the story, and complete the box labeled "In the end…"

4 Use the organizer to encourage discussion.

- ✹ How does the beginning event affect what happened in the middle?

- ✹ When do we meet the main characters?

- ✹ When do we find out about the problem? (if there is one)

- ✹ When is the problem resolved?

- ✹ Do the characters learn anything at the end?

- ✹ When does most of the action take place?

A great book for this organizer is:

Miss Nelson Is Missing by Harry Allard (Scholastic, 1977)

Name: ___Matty___ Date: __May 31__

Beginning...Middle...End

Title: __Miss Nelson Is Missing__

In the beginning…

Miss Nelson is having trouble with her class. The children are misbehaving.

In the middle…

Miss Nelson didn't come to school. Miss Viola Swamp was her sub and she was mean.

In the end…

Miss Nelson came back and the children were glad. Was Miss Swamp really Miss Nelson?

First Graphic Organizers: Reading ● Scholastic Professional Books   39

Tips

✳ Sometimes it is challenging to identify the key points in a story. This organizer helps children focus on the important points. Condensing the story into three main sections encourages children to differentiate between the main points and the details.

✳ Encourage children to use sophisticated words such as *conflict*, *resolution*, and *resolved* as they discuss their work.

Name: _____ Date: _____

Title: _____

In the beginning...

_____
- -
_____
- -
_____
- -
_____

In the middle...

_____
- -
_____
- -
_____
- -
_____

In the end...

_____
- -
_____
- -
_____
- -
_____

An Important Point

Children will identify an important point from a story and write key information supporting the point.

MATERIALS: copies of page 41, pencils

WHEN TO USE: after reading

DIRECTIONS:

1. Have children record the topic and title. Then have them identify a key point from the story. (There may be more than one, but have them focus on one for this activity.) They write it on the lines above the hand.

2. Help children use the book as reference to find three key words or phrases that support the important point. They record each of these points, one on each finger.

3. Use the organizer to encourage discussion:

   ◉ What helped you decide what the important point would be?

   ◉ What is the difference between the index finger and the other fingers?

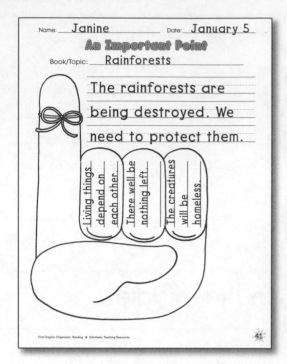

Tips

✳ Try using this with a nonfiction book.

✳ This can be used to help children organize and complete small research projects.

. . . .

A great book for this organizer is:

The Great Kapok Tree
by Lynne Cherry (Harcourt Brace
Jovanovich, Inc., 1990)

Name: _____   Date: _____

An Important Point

Book/Topic: _____

_____
_____
_____
_____
_____
_____
_____

Scoops of Details

Children will identify the main idea of a story, using three details to support their conclusion.

MATERIALS: copies of page 43, pencils, crayons

WHEN TO USE: after reading

DIRECTIONS:

1. Help children determine the main idea of the story and write it in the box at the bottom left.

2. Children fill in the ice cream scoops by writing supporting facts. Children might also draw the supporting facts.

3. Use the organizer to encourage discussion:
   - How do the details support the main idea?
   - How is a cone like a main idea? (it "carries" the details/scoops)
   - How did you decide what the main idea was?

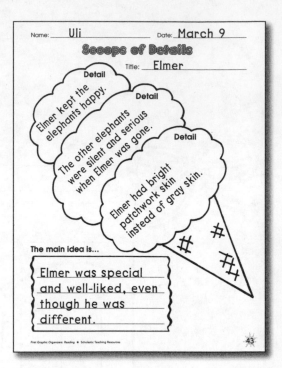

Name: Uli   Date: March 9
Scoops of Details
Title: Elmer

Detail — Elmer kept the elephants happy.

Detail — The other elephants were silent and serious when Elmer was gone.

Detail — Elmer had bright patchwork skin instead of gray skin.

The main idea is...

Elmer was special and well-liked, even though he was different.

First Graphic Organizers: Reading ✳ Scholastic Teaching Resources   43

Tips

✳ Provide the details and have children determine the main idea.

✳ Provide the main idea and have children complete the details.

A great book for this organizer is:

Elmer by David McKee (William Morrow & Company, 1968)

Name: _____ Date: _____

Scoops of Details

Title: _____

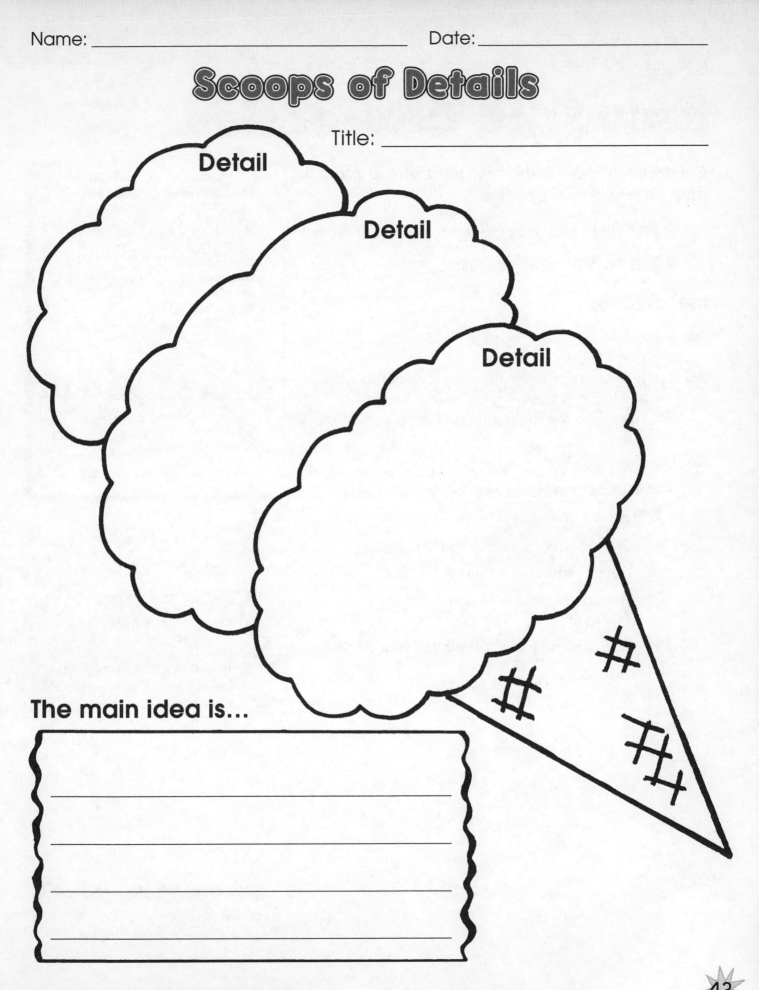

Detail

Detail

Detail

The main idea is…

Main Idea Celebration

Children will identify the main idea of a story and give examples to support it.

MATERIALS: copies of page 45, pencils, crayons

WHEN TO USE: after reading

DIRECTIONS:

1 Have children fill in the title of the book.

2 Help children identify the main idea of the story and record it in the birthday cake. They can also illustrate the main idea on the other side of the page.

3 Have children identify three details that support the main idea and record them in the birthday presents.

4 Use the organizer to encourage discussion:

⚙ How did you choose the main idea?

⚙ How do the details help support the main idea?

⚙ Are there any other details you would add?

Name: Donald   Date: June 4

Main Idea Celebration

Title: Leo the Late Bloomer

MAIN IDEA

When Leo was ready, he would bloom.

Detail
Leo didn't write, read or draw.

Detail
Leo's father watched TV.

Detail
A watched bloomer doesn't bloom.

First Graphic Organizers: Reading ● Scholastic Teaching Resources   45

Tips

✶ Supply the main idea and have children fill in the details.

✶ Supply the details and have the children identify the main idea.

. . . .

A great book for this organizer is:

Leo the Late Bloomer by
Robert Kraus (HarperCollins, 1971)

Name: _____ Date: _____

Main Idea Celebration

Title: _____

MAIN IDEA

Detail

Detail

Detail

The Main Idea Box

Children will identify the main idea of a story, and provide two details that support the main idea.

MATERIALS: copies of page 47, pencils

WHEN TO USE: after reading

DIRECTIONS:

1. Have children record the title at the top of the page.

2. Have children identify the main idea of the story and write the main idea in the crayon box at the top of the page.

3. Then, help them identify two details in the story that help support the main idea. They record these details on the lines under the crayons.

4. Use the organizer to encourage discussion:

   ❂ Why do you think the author wrote this story? (Discuss the author's purpose by noting what the main idea is.)

   ❂ Did the author tell us the main idea directly or did he or she show us the main idea by something that happened in the story?

   ❂ Why are the details important? Do they help us determine the main idea?

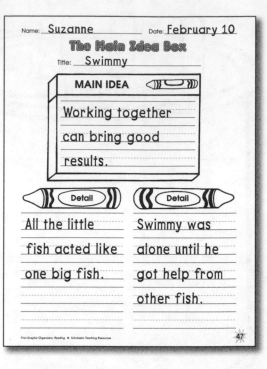

Name: Suzanne   Date: February 10

The Main Idea Box

Title: Swimmy

MAIN IDEA

Working together can bring good results.

Detail — All the little fish acted like one big fish.

Detail — Swimmy was alone until he got help from other fish.

First Graphic Organizers: Reading • Scholastic Teaching Resources   47

Tips

✳ Young children will need many examples and modeling to begin to understand this concept. Provide them with plenty of practice before they complete this organizer on their own.

✳ It may be easier to identify some details first and then use them to determine the main idea.

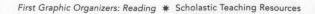

A great book for this organizer is:

Swimmy by Leo Lionni
(Alfred A. Knopf, 1963)

Name: _____ Date: _____

The Main Idea Box

Title: _____

MAIN IDEA

_____
_____
_____
_____
_____
_____

Detail

_____
_____
_____
_____
_____
_____
_____
_____

Detail

_____
_____
_____
_____
_____
_____
_____
_____

Wondrous, Wondrous Words!

Children will find interesting words and phrases in a book and learn about the importance of interesting word choice in reading and writing.

MATERIALS: copies of page 49, pencils, crayons

WHEN TO USE: during reading, after reading

DIRECTIONS:

 Have children record the title.

2 Discuss the author's purpose. Is the author trying to inform or entertain? Children write *to inform* or *to entertain* in the box.

3 Have children identify any words or phrases that struck them as interesting, new or fun. Tell children to choose words or phrases that sound special to them.

 Have children illustrate one of the words or phrases, then write a personal response.

 Use the organizer to encourage discussion:

   ☼ What did the author mean when he or she used that word? How else can you say that?

   ☼ Why did you choose that word or phrase? Was it different? Fun to say? Did you understand it?

Name: Kisha   Date: January 10

Wondrous, Wondrous Words!

Title: Come On, Rain!

Author's Purpose: to entertain

Wondrous Words

it freckles our feet
sizzling like a hot potato
bunched and bulging

Personal Response

I like hot days and rainy days.

First Graphic Organizers: Reading ✳ Scholastic Teaching Resources   49

Tips

✳ Complete this as a class, with you acting as scribe.

✳ Keep a class list of interesting language or wondrous words. It will help children appreciate language and inspire them in their writing.

A great book for this organizer is:

Come On, Rain! by Karen Hesse (Scholastic, 1999)

Wondrous, Wondrous Words!

Title: _____

Author's Purpose } _____
_____

Wondrous Words

_____
_____
_____
_____
_____
_____
_____

Personal Response

_____
_____
_____
_____

Bucket of Words

Children will learn new vocabulary from a story by accessing prior knowledge.

MATERIALS: copies of page 51, pencils, crayons

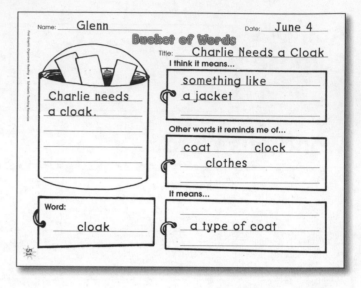

DIRECTIONS:

1 Prior to copying the reproducible, fill in a focus word from a story in the blank box (bottom left). Fill in the bucket with a quote from the book, showing how the word is used in context. Record the title at top. Then, copy the page for each child and distribute.

2 Read the word and the sentence aloud.

3 Ask children to think about what the word means and record their thoughts in the top box. Then ask children to think of any other words the focus word reminds them of, and record their answers in the middle box.

4 Together, guide children to a final conclusion as to the definition of the word using children's responses. Record the final definition in the box labeled, "It means…."

5 Use the organizer to encourage discussion:

⚙ How can we use the story to help us figure out the meaning of a new word?

⚙ What are some other strategies we can use to figure out what a new word means when we are reading a story?

Tips

✳ Use the new word in conversation during the day.

✳ Refer to the vocabulary strategies often. Extend these strategies beyond this specific lesson into everyday situations, to help children continually improve their vocabularies.

. . . .

A great book for this organizer is:

Charlie Needs a Cloak by Tomie dePaola (Simon & Schuster, 1973)

Name: _____

Date: _____

Bucket of Words

Title: _____

I think it means...

Other words it reminds me of...

It means...

Word: _____

I Wonder...

"Wondering" helps children build comprehension by questioning and thinking about what they read, ultimately thinking about a text more thoroughly.

MATERIALS: copies of page 53, pencils, crayons, copy of book read

WHEN TO USE: during reading, after reading

DIRECTIONS:

1. Have children record the title of the story. Read part of the story aloud. (In a chapter book, read at least through chapter two before noting a stop point.) Stop reading at a particular point and record the page number on the line at left.

2. Invite children to wonder about something that happened, predict what might happen, or relate the story to personal experience ("I wonder if it will turn out like the time I..."). Record this information under the corresponding "I Wonder" column.

3. Have children illustrate the "wonderings."

4. Continue reading until the next stop point, then repeat the above. Do the same at the end of the story.

5. Use the organizer to encourage discussion:
   - How did your wonderings change the way you read the rest of the story and thought about its characters?

Tip

- Children might choose the stop points, or the stop points can be chosen at random during reading.

- Fill in the stop point page numbers before you distribute the handout.

. . . .

A great book for this organizer is:

Magic Tree House: Dinosaurs Before Dark by Mary Pope Osborne (Random House, 1992)

Name: _____   Date: _____

I Wonder...

Title: _____

page
_____

page
_____

end
of
story

I wonder...

_____

- -

_____

- -

_____

I wonder...

_____

- -

_____

- -

_____

I wonder...

_____

- -

_____

- -

_____

Question It!

Children will identify important information from the story by answering the "five W" questions (who? what? where? when? why?).

MATERIALS: copies of page 55, pencils, crayons

WHEN TO USE: after reading

DIRECTIONS:

1 Have children record the title.

2 Looking through the book, have children go back and identify the *who, what, where, when,* and *why* of a story. They can fill in the boxes with pictures, words, or both.

3 Use the organizer to encourage discussion:

- What do all of these question words have in common? (All begin with *wh-*.)

- Could any of the question words have several different answers? Why?

- What is another question word? Hint: It begins with H.

Name: Jackie	Date: Sept. 21

Question It!

Title: **Dandelion**

Who?	Dandelion
What?	Dandelion isn't recognized at his friend Jennifer Giraffe's.
Where?	Jennifer Giraffe's house
When?	Saturday afternoon
Why?	Dandelion had fancy hair and his friends didn't recognize him.

First Graphic Organizers: Reading ✳ Scholastic Teaching Resources   55

Tips

✳ Fill in the boxes with pictures for children to label.

✳ Consider filling in the boxes with partial statements and having children complete the sentences.

A great book for this organizer is:

Dandelion by Don Freeman (The Viking Press, Puffin Books, 1964)

Name: _____   Date: _____

Question It!

Title: _____

Who? 	
What?	
Where?	
When?	
Why?	

Let's Compare!

Similar to a Venn Diagram, this organizer allows children to compare and contrast two versions of the same story.

MATERIALS: copies of page 57, pencils

WHEN TO USE: after reading

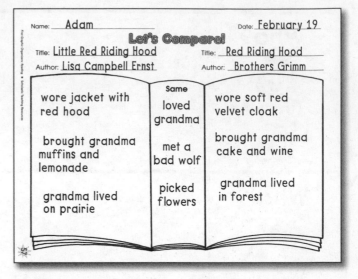

DIRECTIONS:

1. After reading two versions of the same story (such as "Little Red Riding Hood," "Goldilocks," or any familiar tale), record the titles and authors of the books at top.

2. Invite children to think about what was the same and what was different in the stories.

3. Have children record the similarities on the spine of the book. Have children record the differences on the pages of the book.

4. Use the organizer to encourage discussion:

   ◉ Which version did you prefer? Why?

   ◉ Did the differences change the overall plot?

   ◉ What do you think was the biggest difference?

   ◉ What parts of the story do you think are necessary to remain the same in order to keep the original plot?

Tips

✳ Instead of books, try comparing and contrasting a book to a movie or video.

✳ Invite children to write their own version of a familiar tale and compare the two using the organizer.

Great books for this organizer are:

The Random House Book of Fairy Tales adapted by Amy Ehrlich (Random House, 1985)

Little Red Riding Hood: A Newfangled Prairie Tale by Lisa Campbell Ernst (Simon & Schuster, 1995)

56

Name: _____

Date: _____

Let's Compare!

Title: _____

Author: _____

Title: _____

Author: _____

Same

Deep Thinkers

Children will share prior knowledge, ask questions, and make associations based on what they see, hear, and understand before, during, or after reading.

MATERIALS: copies of page 59, pencils

WHEN TO USE: before, during, or after reading

DIRECTIONS:

1 Decide when you are going to use the organizer: before, during, or after reading. Children can then complete the top portion of the organizer by circling the appropriate time: before, during, or after, and filling in the title of the book.

2 Have children brainstorm what they think about when presented with the topic. Have them record their responses in the given columns. Encourage them to write words, ask questions, or make predictions. They can use words, pictures, or sentences.

3 Use the organizer to encourage discussion:
- What did you see or hear that made you respond as you did?
- Were your questions answered by reading the story?

Name: **Jack**   Date: **September 7**

Deep Thinkers

Write any words, phrases, or questions that come to mind before, during, or after reading.

Title: **The Mitten**

Words/Phrases	Questions/Predictions
winter	Whose mitten is it?
snow	What will the animals do with the mitten?
cold	
curious	Why is there only one?
gloves	The mitten will find its owner.
scarf	

Tips

* Consider using this organizer for nonfiction or poetry as well.

* Have children complete this organizer prior to reading and then right after reading. Then use both organizers and discuss how the story impacts what they thought about and how their thinking changed.

A great book for this organizer is:

The Mitten by Jan Brett (G. P. Putnam's Sons, 1989)

Name: _____

Date: _____

Deep Thinkers

Write any words, phrases, or questions that come to mind before, during, or after reading.

Title: _____

Words/Phrases

Questions/Predictions

What It Means to Me

Children choose a specific incident or theme from a story and connect it to their lives.

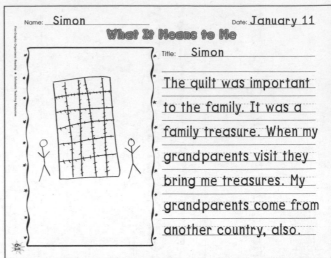

> Name: **Simon**   Date: **January 11**
> ## What It Means to Me
> Title: **Simon**
>
> The quilt was important to the family. It was a family treasure. When my grandparents visit they bring me treasures. My grandparents come from another country, also.

MATERIALS: copies of page 61, pencils, crayons

WHEN TO USE: after reading

DIRECTIONS:

1. Have children record the title.

2. Then, have children write a sentence about something in the story that reminded them of their own lives. It can be a character, an action or event, the problem, the setting, or anything that seems important to them.

3. Have children write a sentence about how the topic relates to their lives. If there is no connection, have them write about the situation and how they felt as they read.

4. Let children illustrate their response.

5. Use the organizer to encourage discussion:

   ☉ Do you think the same story can mean different things to different people?

   ☉ How does your experience relate to the character's experience? Are there similarities or differences?

Tip

✴ Some children may feel more comfortable illustrating first and then writing about their illustration. Some children may illustrate only and then describe their illustration. Encourage all responses.

. . . .

A great book for this organizer is:
The Keeping Quilt by Patricia Polacco (Simon & Schuster, 1988)

Name: _____

Date: _____

What It Means to Me

Title: _____

All Aboard!

Children will complete three sections on a train in response to what they've read.

MATERIALS: copies of page 63, pencils, crayons

WHEN TO USE: after reading

DIRECTIONS:

1 Have children record the title and then fill in the three boxes at the top of each train car. They are blank so you can choose how to direct the activity:

- ☉ characters/problem/solution
- ☉ beginning/middle/end
- ☉ time/place/characters
- ☉ character's problem/what I would have done/what the character did in the end

In the example above, the train headings are beginning, middle, and end.

2 Have the children complete each section, writing and/or drawing in the spaces on each train car.

3 Use the organizer to encourage discussion:

- ☉ What is the relationship between the train cars?
- ☉ What are some other ways you could fill in the three headings?

Tip

✱ When reviewing the story, especially beginning, middle, and end, try to show the relationship between the parts, reinforcing the transitions and the key points. It is difficult to summarize a story succinctly into three parts, even for older children!

A great book for this organizer is:

Berlioz the Bear by Jan Brett (G. P. Putnam's Sons, 1991)

Name: _____

Date: _____

All Aboard!

Title: _____

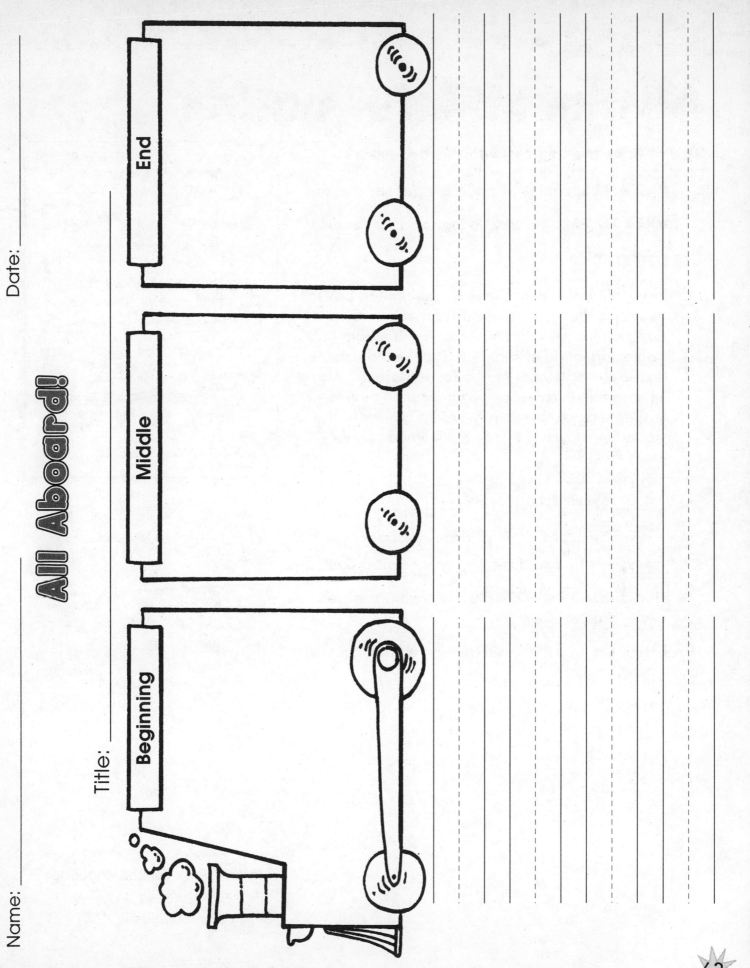

Beginning

Middle

End

Stroke of Information

The options are endless with this organizer!

MATERIALS: copies of page 65, pencils, crayons

WHEN TO USE: before, during, or after reading

DIRECTIONS:

1 Have children record the title. Use the top box to direct children how to use this organizer. Write a question for them to answer, or use it to identify beginning, middle, and end. Copy and distribute. (In the example at right, the focus is identifying what the main character has learned in the story. In this instance, children will identify parts of the story that show what Little Bill learned.) Other ideas include:

  ❂ character's name and three traits

  ❂ list of three different settings of story

  ❂ problem and three possible solutions

  ❂ story title and three personal connections

2 Have the children write or draw their response in each "brushstroke."

3 Discussion questions will depend on the focus of the activity.

Name: Brook   Date: May 5
Stroke of Information
Title: My Big Lie

What did Little Bill learn?

It isn't good to lie.

It's hard to admit when you've done something wrong.

He's lucky because his mom and dad trust him.

First Graphic Organizers: Reading • Scholastic Teaching Resources   65

Tip

✳ This organizer can also be used with nonfiction and poetry.

A great book for this organizer is:

Little Bill: My Big Lie by Bill Cosby (Scholastic, 1999)

Stroke of Information

Title: _____

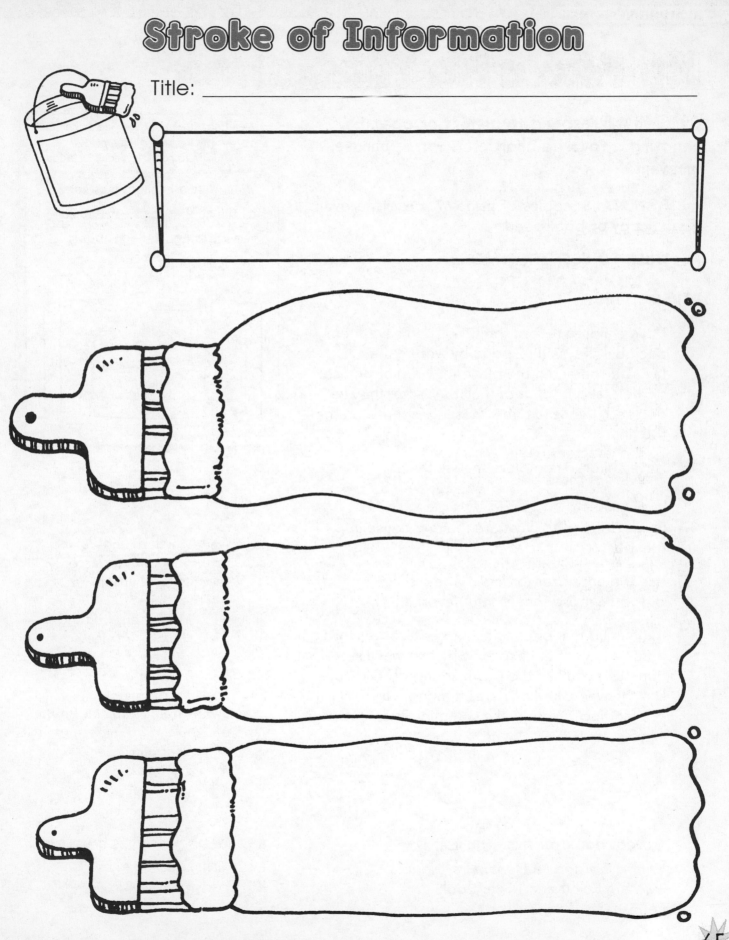

My Favorite Things

Children will respond to a story or poem by choosing a favorite character, word, phrase, or event.

MATERIALS: copies of page 67, pencils, crayons, copy of book read

WHEN TO USE: after reading

DIRECTIONS:

1 Have children record the title. Then have them decide if they will respond by writing their favorite character, their favorite word or phrase, or their favorite part of the story. After they have decided, they circle the chosen response on the top line.

2 Have children complete the sentence:

My favorite _____ was…

3 Invite children to illustrate their response in the box.

4 Use the organizer to encourage discussion. (*Why did you choose that as your favorite…?*)

5 If the child responds to his or her favorite word or phrase, have them explain why that word stood out. "Did you like the way it sounded? Did you like the way it looked? Was it a new word? Was it challenging? Did it make you think of something else?"

Name: Leo   Date: September 28

My Favorite Things

Title: Wilfrid Gordon McDonald Partridge

My favorite   character   word   (part)   was…

When Wilfrid brought Miss Nancy all the cool things so she could remember again. He probably felt really good.

shells
egg

First Graphic Organizers: Reading ✳ Scholastic Teaching Resources   67

Tips

✳ Once children understand how to identify a personal favorite (a character, a word, or a part), encourage them to discuss their choices. For instance, *I see Wilfrid giving Miss Nancy her memory back is your favorite part. What did you think about, or how did you feel, when Miss Nancy got her memory back?*

. . . .

A great book for this organizer is:

Wilfrid Gordon McDonald Partridge by Mem Fox (Kane/Miller Book Publishers, 1985)

Name: _____ Date: _____

My Favorite Things

Title: _____

My favorite   character   word   part   was...

_____
- -
_____
- -
_____
- -
_____
- -
_____

Nonfiction News

After reading a nonfiction text, children will identify and illustrate two key facts.

MATERIALS: copies of page 69, pencils, crayons, sticky notes

WHEN TO USE: after reading

DIRECTIONS:

1 Read a nonfiction text. Have children fill in the topic and title on the lines at the top of the page. (Encourage children to use sticky notes to mark important information as they read, so they can easily find the facts later.)

2 Help children identify two key facts from the given text and write them on the lines.

3 Have children illustrate the facts.

4 Use the organizer to encourage discussion:

☀ Using question words *who, what, where, when* and *why* have children discuss what they have learned. This information can be recorded and used as reference for the class. For example:
  What do snails have on their tongues?
  Where do snails have eyes?

Name: Arthur   *Date:* Nov. 2

Nonfiction News

Topic: Snails

Title: The Snail's Spell

Fact 1	Fact 2
Snails have teeth on their tongues.	Snails have eyes on the tips of their feelers.

teeth

eyes

First Graphic Organizers: Reading ● Scholastic Teaching Resources 69

Tips

✱ Provide the children with the organizer prior to reading to set the purpose. Explain that children will be looking for facts.

✱ Prior to reading, use a KWL, web or brainstorming to help children focus on the topic.

✱ Use a big book and complete the organizer as a class.

✱ Provide one illustration or fact on the handout to get children started.

A great book for this organizer is:

The Snail's Spell by Joanne Ryder (Penguin, 1982)

Name: _____   Date: _____

Nonfiction News

Topic: _____

Title: _____

Fact 1	Fact 2
_____	_____
- - - - - - - - - - - - - - - - - -	- - - - - - - - - - - - - - - - - -
_____	_____
- - - - - - - - - - - - - - - - - -	- - - - - - - - - - - - - - - - - -
_____	_____
- - - - - - - - - - - - - - - - - -	- - - - - - - - - - - - - - - - - -
_____	_____
- - - - - - - - - - - - - - - - - -	- - - - - - - - - - - - - - - - - -
_____	_____
- - - - - - - - - - - - - - - - - -	- - - - - - - - - - - - - - - - - -
_____	_____

Nonfiction Vocabulary

Children will focus on two key words based on a nonfiction selection.

MATERIALS: copies of page 71, pencils, crayons

WHEN TO USE: during reading, after reading

DIRECTIONS:

1 Have children write the title on the top lines. (They should include the topic if it is not in the title.)

2 On each line, children write a new word from the text.

3 Help children determine the meaning of each word and write each definition underneath. Use the book as a reference.

4 Use the illustration boxes to draw pictures that explain each word.

5 Use the organizer to encourage discussion:

- Can you use one of the new words in a sentence?

- How do your pictures help teach the meanings of the words?

Name: Eva   Date: Jan. 20

Nonfiction Vocabulary

Title: Ducks!

Word	Word
preening	brood
Definition	**Definition**
A duck oils its	A group of
feathers with	ducklings
waxy oil. This is	(baby ducks)
called preening.	

First Graphic Organizers: Reading ✷ Scholastic Teaching Resources   71

Tips

✷ Fill in the words prior to distributing the organizers.

✷ Depending on reading level, children can identify their own words as they read.

✷ Consider assigning small groups of children a different set of words using the same book or topic. Each group can share their information so that the class is exposed to many new words and meanings.

. . . .

A great book for this organizer is:
Ducks! by Gail Gibbons (Holiday House, 2001)

Nonfiction Vocabulary

Title: _____

Word	Word
_____	_____
- - - - - - - - - - - -	- - - - - - - - - - - -
_____	_____

Definition	**Definition**
_____	_____
- - - - - - - - - - - -	- - - - - - - - - - - -
_____	_____
- - - - - - - - - - - -	- - - - - - - - - - - -
_____	_____
_____	_____
_____	_____
- - - - - - - - - - - -	- - - - - - - - - - - -
_____	_____

Additional Resources

Bromley, Karen, Linda Irwin-DeVitis, and Marcia Modlo. *Graphic Organizers: Visual Strategies for Active Learning*. New York: Scholastic, 1995.

Hyerle, David. *A Field Guide to Using Visual Tools*. Alexandria: Association for Supervision and Curriculum Development, 2000.

Keene, Ellin Oliver, and Susan Zimmermann. *Mosiac of Thought: Teaching Comprehension in a Reader's Workshop*. Portsmouth: Heinemann, 1997.

Levine, Mel. *Educational Care*. Cambridge: Educators Publishing Service, Inc., 1994.

Levine, Mel. *A Mind At A Time*. New York: Simon & Schuster, 2002.

Murray, Donald M. *Picturing Learning: Artists and Writers in the Classroom*. Portsmouth: Heinemann, 1994. vii.